PREHISTORIC BRITAIN

FROM THE AIR

PREHISTORIC BRITAIN

FROM THE AIR

TEXT BY JANET AND COLIN BORD

PHOTOGRAPHY BY JASON HAWKES

Trafalgar Square Publishing

Shetland Is.

Orkney Is.

Grey Cairns of Camster
Hill o'Many Stanes

Knockfarrel
Dun Beag
•Clava Cairns
Dun Troddan
Dun Telve
•Loanhead
Easter Aquhorthies

Brown Caterthun
White Caterthun

Kilmartin

Traprain Law

Yeavering Bell

Torhouse •Cairnholy

Long Meg and her Daughters
•Castlerigg

•Swinside

Devil's Arrows

Lanyon Quoit
Men-an-Tol
Carn Gluze •Chysauster
Carn Euny •Boscawen-un
Merry Maidens

Din Lligwy
Gop Cairn
Mam Tor
Creswell Crags
Bryn Celli Ddu •Pen-y-Gaer
Pen-y-cloddiau
Arbor Low
Capel Garmon •Moel Arthur
Tre'r Ceiri •Caer Euni •Dinas Bran
Moel-ty-Uchaf •Caer Drewyn
Dyffryn Ardudwy •Old Oswestry
Craig Rhiwarth
Burrough Hill

Caer Caradoc
Grimes Graves

Croft Ambrey

Pentre Ifan •Arthur's Stone •Herefordshire Beacon
Carreg Samson •Foel Trigarn •Belas Knap •Rollright Stones
The Sanctuary •Wayland's Smithy
Avebury •Uffington Castle
Arthur's Stone •Windmill Hill •Uffington White Horse
West Kennet Avenue •Barbury Castle
Tinkinswood •Bratton Castle •Seven Barrows
Stanton Drew •Silbury Hill
Stoney Littleton •Cley Hill •Beacon Hill
Winterbourne Stoke •Stonehenge
Yarnbury Castle •Figsbury Ring
South Cadbury Castle •Normanton Down •Cissbury Ring
•Knowlton Circles
Hambledon Hill •Dorset Cursus •Long Man of Wilmington
Hembury Castle •Badbury Rings
Pilsdon Pen •Hod Hill
Grimspound •Eggardon Hill •Cerne Abbas Giant
Merrivale
The Hurlers •Maiden Castle

0   50   100 Miles

0   50   100   150 Kilometre

CONTENTS

INTRODUCTION

As the twentieth century draws to a close, Britain seems in some respects to have taken on the appearance of a huge heritage theme park. 'Stately homes' are no longer family homes, but grand museums with interiors frozen in time; ruined abbeys are tidied up – the stonework neatly repaired, the nettles removed, the grass shorn, and the souvenir shop opened; while pseudo-historical sites have sprung up depicting themes like the Celtic world, or the King Arthur story. It's good to be aware of the past, but perhaps not so good to be fed a fantasized version of it. However well-intentioned all the guardians of these historical sites may be, it has proved impossible for any of them to truly recapture what it feels like to be living in that particular time. The lives of people even only a century ago are in many ways so different from ours that we can never experience them, only look on and imagine. Inevitably the passage of time throws up in its wake an impenetrable barrier.

If the life of rich man and peasant in the last few hundred years can only be glimpsed and never experienced, how much more difficult it is to attempt to go back even further, to the time before events were recorded in writing – to prehistory. All the information that has been gained about the Prehistoric Era – which ended very approximately with the arrival of the Romans in Britain and the birth of Christ, when BC gave way to AD around 2,000 years ago – has been based on evidence collected by antiquarians and archaeologists from long-buried sites. The picture that has been painstakingly built up over the years since archaeology became a scientific activity, roughly during the last 100 years, has come about as a result of comparison, interpretation, inspiration and guesswork. The very uncertainty of the picture means that it changes with each new generation, prehistory being reinvented every quarter-century

or so. The artefacts that have been discovered remain constant, as do the structural remains, but the scenario to which they give life is constantly, subtly, changing.

However, the timescale of prehistory is roughly this: the earliest evidence of humans living in what is now Britain dates back around 400,000 years, to the period now known as the Old Stone Age. But we must come forward many thousands of years, to the New Stone Age, before we can see any identifiable traces of our ancestors on the British landscape. The New Stone Age ran from approximately 4000 BC to 2300 BC (remember that all the dates and names are modern inventions), and the kinds of landscape features that still survive from that time are labelled as causewayed camps, henges, chambered tombs and long barrows. Around 2300 BC the New Stone Age gave way to the Bronze Age, during which time stone circles and standing stones were erected, together with round barrows and cairns. The Iron Age began around 750 BC, but the people of the time would have noticed little change, other than that bronze was replaced by iron. Hillforts date from the Iron Age, an early form of landscape engineering that seems to have taken place on most prominent hilltops.

This brief description of the structural remains of 4,000 years of human occupation of Britain is acutely inadequate in giving a real picture of what was going on. And it's worth emphasizing again that 2–6,000 years after the events, one can only surmise what really happened. But the wealth of structural remains, which still lie scattered throughout Britain after so many years, is an indication that our prehistoric ancestors were as active in construction as is modern man. There is much of prehistoric Britain left for the twentieth-century visitor to explore: 1,000 megalithic tombs,

30,000–40,000 round barrows in England alone, over 900 stone circles, around 3,000 hillforts, and countless thousands of standing stones still survive. Most people are not aware of this huge legacy: only Stonehenge has penetrated the national consciousness.

Many people who have visited Stonehenge, expecting something spectacular, have been disappointed: it seems smaller that they imagined it would be, and the trappings of tourism definitely detract from the atmosphere. It seems that all this will change in the not-too-distant future, as a new environment for Britain's major prehistoric site is planned. But meanwhile it is not a good ambassador for the rest of the sites, which is a pity, because so many of them, especially the more remote which you have to tramp across empty moorland to find, are most definitely overflowing with atmosphere. No matter that they often consist of no more than a few big stones stuck into the ground. Untouched by the let's-tidy-up mentality, with nettles aplenty and only sheep to keep watch, the vast majority of Britain's prehistoric sites are poignant relics of a past we can hardly begin to imagine. Time has peopled them with ghosts of past events, and legends

Uffington White Horse, Oxfordshire

describe what might once have happened there. All as fanciful as the archaeologists' speculations, no doubt, but no less interesting for that.

The modern traveller cocooned in his horseless carriage is rarely aware of the history of the landscape he so effortlessly passes through; but the aerial traveller can see so much more of the vast panorama that is Britain, and when his eye becomes accustomed to the significance of all the bumps and hollows, he finds himself looking not at the landscape of the late twentieth century, but at a landscape fashioned by many generations of country people. Considering how each generation has made its own changes to the environment, it is amazing that so many of prehistoric man's structures have survived. Perhaps the fact that they became overlaid with superstition may have helped: it was often believed to be dangerous to interfere with such places. But whatever the reason, thankfully they have survived, as Jason Hawkes's fine photographs make very clear. And seen from this unusual perspective, the sites and structures take on a new significance, for they can be seen not in isolation but as part of a larger landscape, as for example at Stonehenge, where so many different monuments form an important ceremonial network.

It is still possible to escape from 'Heritage Britain', and to find one's way into the real historical and ancient Britain. The main requirements are a good guidebook, an Ordnance Survey map, determination and imagination. But once you are off the beaten track on some wild moorland, far from the crowds and coach parks, you will find that the search for the past can be a rewarding path to travel.

Beacon Hill Hillfort, Hampshire

ENGLAND

In our small island we have a great variety of landscape – mountains and valleys, rocky crags and fertile plains – and even in England alone this variation is apparent. The types of prehistoric sites that have survived also vary according to the nature of the landscape: as might be expected, in the rocky areas the structures are largely built of stones, while in the flat lands with a shortage of large stones, earth was used. Also, the fertile lowlands have been farmed more intensively which has resulted in the disappearance of many prehistoric structures – though it is surprising how much can be deduced from aerial photographs, and in dry weather the outlines of former structures are clearly defined by variations in crop growth caused by ancient disturbances to the soil. Once this effect was realized, aerial archaeology has become very important in helping to expand our knowledge of how England was settled, and as new settlements are constantly being discovered, it is apparent that even in prehistoric times there was no part of England that was not inhabited and farmed. The upland regions, which can today seem rather inhospitable to farming, were also well populated, which tells us that either the people were hardier in the past, or the weather was better, or maybe both!

Although some major monuments survive – Stonehenge and Avebury are obvious examples – it is probable that other major monuments, at one time equally important, have been lost. We should also remember that the prehistoric monuments we see today cover a long period: the Iron Age hillforts date from around 2,500 years after the long barrows.

All types of sites are to be found in England, but the most numerous are burial chambers, starting with the elaborate earthen long barrows containing stone chambers (West Kennet and Stoney Littleton are fine examples) of around 3500 BC and ending with the simpler earthen round barrow cemeteries (such as Winterbourne Stoke and Normanton Down). Also very numerous are the hillforts, which are probably the most impressive structures to view from the air, with their bank-and-ditch fortifications winding sinuously around prominent hilltops. (Maiden Castle and Herefordshire Beacon are fine examples.)

Stone circles and standing stones are also numerous, especially in the south-west, but look less impressive from the air than at ground level. Aerial views serve to show their relationship to the surrounding landscape (Stonehenge especially is only part of a much larger ceremonial landscape), and in the case of more complex monuments such as henges with stones an aerial view shows the overall pattern which cannot be properly appreciated from the ground (for example, at Avebury).

Another category of monument which is best seen from the air is the hill figure, a curious survival which has caused considerable controversy. Three major examples survive in England: the Cerne Abbas Giant, The Long Man of Wilmington, and the Uffington White Horse. Why our ancestors felt the urge to create huge figures on chalk hillsides remains a mystery – and especially with regard to the Uffington White Horse, which can only be properly seen from the air.

Caer Caradoc
Hillfort, Shropshire

Knowlton Henge,
Dorset

Arbor Low Henge, Derbyshire

Arbor Low is classed as a 'henge monument': its defining banks and ditches were clearly not intended to keep invaders out physically, and no trace of settlement has been found, so therefore the enclosure must have been intended as a meeting place of some kind, possibly for seasonal ceremonies and rituals. Beyond that, little can be deduced. In 1848 antiquarian Thomas Bateman wrote: 'Were it not for a few stone walls which intervene in the foreground, the solitude of the place and the boundless views are such as almost carry the observer back through a multitude of centuries and make him believe that he sees the same view and the same state of things as existed in the days of the architects of this once holy place.' Can this be true? The major puzzle at Arbor Low is the stone circle. The large white limestone blocks are all lying flat, and no trace of holes has been found. So did they ever stand upright? They could have been propped up by other stones – or maybe they were always recumbent. Another mystery is the low earth bank which can be seen in the centre of the photograph, heading out from the henge. It was apparently constructed at the same time as the henge, but for what purpose?

In the bank of the henge at the left is a damaged tumulus, in which Thomas Bateman found a stone box containing burnt human bones and two clay urns or food vessels. This tumulus is thought to date from the Bronze Age, some hundreds of years after the henge was in use. Not far away, and not visible in the photograph, is another tumulus known as Gib Hill, which is still 16.5 feet (5 metres) high. Again Thomas Bateman was the one to discover its contents, a small urn or food vessel and some burnt human bones inside a stone container. The presence of these burial structures shows that the place was still considered sacred many years after it had ceased to be used for its original purpose. Similar examples of uninterrupted use have continued into the present millennium, with Christian churches often being built on the sacred sites of former times.

Arthur's Stone Chambered Tomb, Hereford & Worcester
It is unfortunate that structures such as this, a Neolithic burial chamber on the Welsh border, should need to be isolated from their surroundings by fences and walls, presumably for protection from vehicles and animals. Or does the wall or fence represent a symbolic separation? An interpretation being: this structure within the wall represents history, and so stands apart from the everyday life going on outside.

The stones forming this Neolithic chambered tomb were erected around 5,000 years ago. At left can be seen the remains of a 15-foot (4.5-metre) passageway leading into the tomb, the chamber itself still

roofed by a single large stone. The whole structure would originally have

been covered by an earth mound. The tomb is known as Arthur's Stone, Arthur, of course, being the legendary King Arthur, and there are several tales that link him with this place. A king or a giant killed by Arthur is buried here; or Arthur himself was buried here, the stones marking the site of his tomb. A small stone pitted with 'cup marks' is said to lie nearby. The cups were made by the giant's elbows as he fell; or else they were made by Arthur's knees as he knelt to pray. There has always been – and still is – a need for heroes, and King Arthur has endured as a favourite focus for hero worship.

Avebury Henge, Wiltshire
The village of Avebury is enclosed by the still impressive outer bank and ditch of a Neolithic henge monument. This unique site covers an area of 28 acres (11 hectares) and must have been amazing to behold when it was newly built. Close by are the equally amazing Silbury Hill and West Kennet long barrow (see pp 82 and 99). The outer bank at Avebury is nearly a mile around and its height was originally 55 feet (17 metres) from ditch bottom to bank top – it is still very impressive. It has been estimated that the construction of the Avebury enclosure would have taken some 1,500,000 man-hours.

Inside the enclosure there were originally three stone circles, the largest following the line of the ditch and originally containing around 100 stones. The largest surviving stone is 15 feet (4.4 metres) tall, with a further 4 feet (1.2 metres) below ground. The surviving section of this circle can be seen in the photograph, as can a few other stones which were part of the two smaller inner circles. Many of the stones were smashed in the seventeenth and eighteenth centuries, but some were buried in the fourteenth century, then dug up and re-erected in the 1930s. There may well be more buried stones awaiting rediscovery; but in addition to the loss of stones smashed, others were taken to build the houses of Avebury.

Pieces of pottery found in the circle indicate that Avebury was in use over a period of about 1,000 years from around 2600 BC to 1600 BC, but what it was used for is unknown. Most people agree that ceremonies of some kind were conducted in henges, but beyond that all is conjecture – and there has been plenty of that! Some people have seen a possible significance in the shape of the stones: tall pillar shapes and broad diamond shapes were used alternately, and these may have represented male and female, suggesting that Avebury's rituals had something to do with fertility. Two stone avenues led out from the henge, which were possible processional ways. The West Kennet Avenue has been partially restored at the Avebury end. Originally 100 pairs of stones formed an avenue 1.5 miles (2.4 kilometres) long, linking Avebury henge with a small site known as The Sanctuary (see p. 82).

Over 4,000 years after Avebury was in use, we are very much in the dark as to what went on there, but it seems sensible to assume that there were large-scale occasions attended by most of the people who lived in the area, and that those events related to the most important aspects of life, both of the people and of the land which supported them. So seasonal rites, such as the arrival of spring, would have been celebrated, as would matters of tribal significance, such as the births and deaths of important people. Probably, just like people today, they found many reasons for a celebration, a coming-together to reinforce their sense of community.

Badbury Rings Hillfort, Dorset

Three chalk banks and ditches enclose 18 acres (7.3 hectares) at Badbury Rings, a fine Iron Age fort about which not much is known because it has not yet been excavated. Two Roman roads cross less than 200 metres north-east of the fort, and also close by is a group of round barrows, possibly Bronze Age. Although Badbury Rings has a silent history, folklore has identified it as Mount Badon, the place where King Arthur defeated the Saxons in a battle in AD 518. Another tradition tells that King Arthur lived on after death in the form of a raven in the wood inside the fort.

Barbury Castle Hillfort,
Wiltshire

Situated on the edge of the
Marlborough Downs, Barbury Castle
is perhaps the most atmospheric of
Wiltshire's hillforts. Enclosing an
area of 12 acres (4.7 hectares), its
defensive banks and ditches are still
impressive, as the photograph
shows. It also clearly highlights that
there were entrances on both the
east and west faces. The fort was
occupied during the Iron Age, and
aerial photography has revealed
traces of huts and storage pits,
while items such as jewellery and
chariot fittings have been dug up.
As with some other sites illustrated
in this book, such as Wayland's
Smithy and Uffington Castle,
Barbury Castle is skirted by the
ancient track, The Ridgeway, which
runs along the edge of the downs
just below the hillfort.

Beacon Hill Hillfort, Hampshire

Shaped like an hourglass astride the top of Beacon Hill, the Iron Age hillfort still has an impressive defensive ditch and banks. Fifteen hut sites have been identified in the fort, with animal bones and pottery found there, while smaller hollows probably mark the site of storage pits. The discoverer of Tutankhamun's tomb, Lord Carnarvon, was a former owner of the hill, and has his grave in the fenced-off, south-west corner of the fort.

Belas Knap Long Barrow, Gloucestershire

Neatly packaged in a drystone-wall enclosure high up in the Cotswolds is an intriguing Neolithic long barrow, known as Belas Knap (meaning Beacon Mound). It is intriguing because what appears to be the main entrance to the tomb, at the broadest end, is nothing of the sort. It is a false entrance, presumably designed to fool those who would rob the tomb of its contents; or perhaps to outwit evil spirits. The burials were actually placed in three or four small, stone-built chambers in the sides of the long earth mound, and in these chambers archaeologists have found the remains of thirty burials. Some children's bones and a man's skull were also placed behind the false entrance. It would be fascinating to know the details of the rituals that must have been performed at this important place, but as it all happened over 5,000 years ago, we have no record at all of what went on.

Boscawen-un Stone Circle, Cornwall

Difficult to find and tucked away from the surrounding fields in a circular enclosure, Boscawen-un stone circle is one of Cornwall's most atmospheric prehistoric sites. There would originally have been twenty stones making up the circle, but only nineteen now survive. One of them is different from the rest, being a large white quartz block. Also unusual is the leaning central stone: if it was ever upright, it would have stood 8 feet (2.4 metres) high. A link between these two stones has been suggested, with the square quartz stone representing the female element, and the thin, leaning stone the male element. Numerous possibilities have been put forward to explain this circle's significance. A late medieval Welsh tradition calls it one of the three main Druid meeting places in Britain, while more recently it has been found to have seven leys (alignments of ancient sites) running through it.

Bratton Castle and Westbury White Horse, Wiltshire

Inside the Iron Age hillfort known as Bratton Castle is a Neolithic long barrow 230 feet (70 metres) long, and since this predates the fort by around 2,500 years, the fort builders presumably recognized its religious significance, and it may even have been the focal point of their enclosure. The barrow has suffered from various attempts to excavate it, these digs revealing iron objects, urns and some burials. Inside the fort itself, quern stones (for grinding flour) and a pile of large pebbles, which may have been intended as sling-stones, have been found.

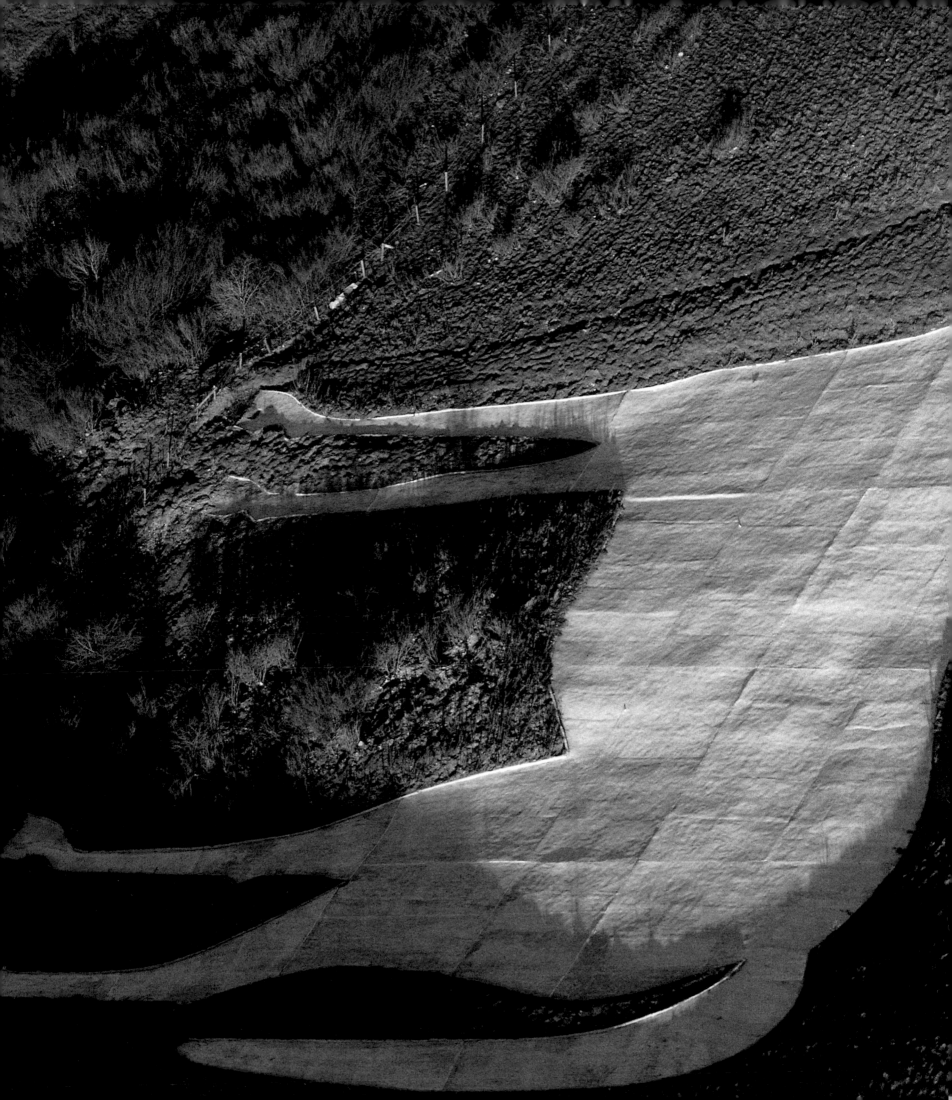

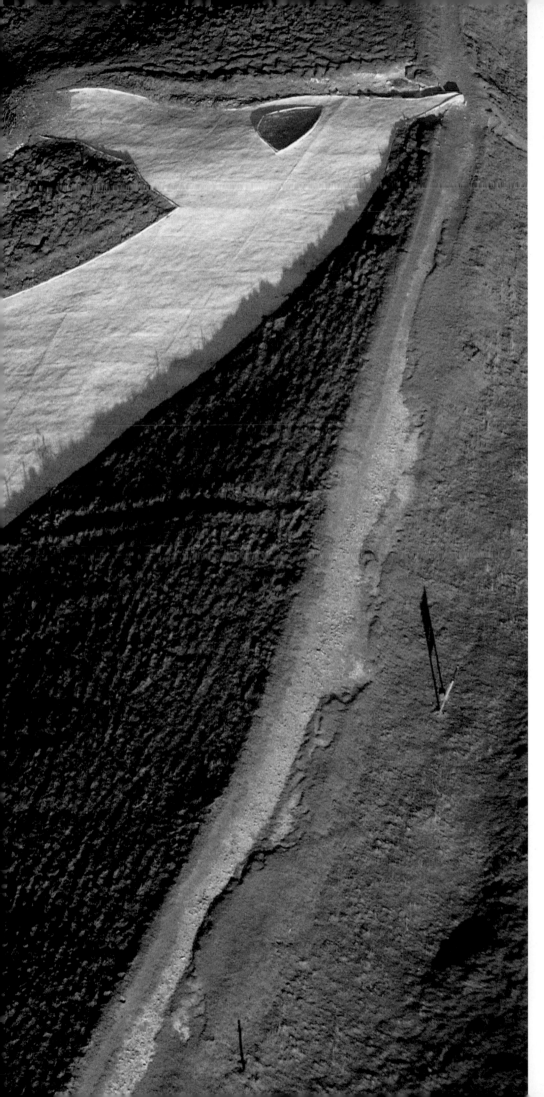

Just outside the rampart of the fort at the western end is one of Wiltshire's chalk figures, the Westbury White Horse. The horse we see today dates only from 1778 when an earlier horse was remodelled. A drawing of the original animal shows a strange creature with a crescent moon on the end of its long, thin tail; it also faced in the opposite direction. It was believed to have been made in AD 878 to celebrate one of King Alfred's battle victories, though the truth of this is uncertain.

Burrough Hill Hillfort, Leicestershire

Judging by the domestic rubbish found when Burrough Hill Iron Age hillfort was investigated by archaeologists, the fort was occupied for several centuries from around the second century BC. Pig, sheep, cow and horse bones were found, together with pottery and querns for grinding grain by hand. Even after it was abandoned as a settlement, the fort continued its use as a gathering place for fairs and festivals. In 1873 the Grand National was even held there, and the fort has also been used for steeple-chasing. Some time during the last century, during a violent blizzard, the village schoolmaster was lost in the fort. His violin was found two days later, and it was feared that he had died, but a search party which went out the next day found him in the snow, amazingly still alive and little the worse for his ordeal.

Caer Caradoc Hillfort, Shropshire

Caer Caradoc Hill rises up from the valley which shelters the village of Church Stretton; the western side of this valley is dominated by the Long Mynd, high moorland giving a hint of the Welsh mountains beyond. Hilltops like Caer Caradoc would have been ideal lookout points, where camps were set up using, wherever possible, the natural rock outcrops to strengthen the man-made defences of stone walls, banks and ditches.

The name Caer Caradoc tells us that this fort (*caer* in Welsh) was built by Caratacus, an early English king who led the opposition to the Roman invasion in AD 43 and was defeated by them somewhere in mid-Wales in AD 51. Folklore persists in linking these events with Caer Caradoc: there was said to be a cave on the steepest face of the hill, where the King hid from his enemies after his defeat. But in reality there is no hard evidence that this hill played any part in these events.

Carn Euny Iron Age Village, Cornwall

Cornwall's most south-westerly peninsula is the ideal haunt for anyone who wants to visit as many prehistoric sites as possible within a small area. At first sight, this stony landscape reaching down twisty lanes doesn't resemble any of the other sites illustrated in this book: it's clearly neither a hillfort, a stone circle nor a burial mound. In fact, Carn Euny is an Iron Age village, and what can be seen are the remains of stone huts clustered together. Details such as hearths, post-holes and drains with stone covers can be found inside the huts; but the most intriguing structure here is the fogou, an underground chamber about 65 feet (20 metres) long. The purpose of this and other fogous found elsewhere is not known, though numerous suggestions for its use have been put forward, including cattle shed, food store or hiding place. Or it may have been a spiritual place where religious rituals were performed: the fogou may have symbolized the womb of the Great Earth Mother. Whatever its true purpose, the fogou at Carn Euny is particularly impressive, as too is the circular stone chamber at one end of it.

Carn Gluze Barrow, Cornwall

Carn Gluze (also known as Ballowal Barrow), sited close to the sea in south-west Cornwall, is a burial site with a complex construction history. Archaeologists have suggested that it may have been in use as a shrine for around 1,000 years in the Bronze Age. One finding which leads to this possibility was a pit 7 feet (2.1 metres) deep, which was dug into the bedrock and contained no burials. Was it perhaps a symbolic route into the underworld? Four small stone cists stood around the top, containing small pots which possibly held food offerings. A large stone cairn over 30 feet (9 metres) high was built over the site: it now survives to a height of 12 feet (3.6 metres) only. Cremated human bones and pieces of pottery have been found in the cairn, suggesting that the rituals performed here were concerned with death, but beyond that nothing certain is known. Traditions of fairies dancing and lights seen by nineteenth-century miners on their way home from work may be folk memories of the rituals once performed here.

Castlerigg Stone Circle, Cumbria

As the photograph shows, the setting of Castlerigg stone circle is a dramatic one, and appears even more so when you are there, in a natural amphitheatre formed by the surrounding hills. The circle too is impressive: the thirty-eight surviving stones (once forty-two) stand no more than 5 feet (1.5 metres) tall, except for the two taller ones at the north-east entrance, but form a powerful presence. The rectangular setting of stones (at present fenced in, but not normally so) is puzzling, but probably has something to do with the original purpose of the circle which may have involved the calculation of significant times of year, the turning points. At such times ceremonies and festivities have been held throughout Britain for centuries up until the present day, and very likely were also held in prehistoric times. This could be one of the earliest stone circles in Europe, possibly erected around 3200 BC. It has remained a popular spot therefore for over 5,000 years. If you want to see it at its most dramatic, when mountains, stones and weather come together to create a powerful experience, visit it at dusk or dawn when the weather is active: above all, avoid a hot and still summer's afternoon when the atmosphere will be flat and the circle alive with visitors.

Cerne Abbas Giant, Dorset

Argument rages as to who created the Cerne Abbas Giant, and when – and also, of course, who he was intended to represent. The first written mention of him was in 1751, but it seems likely that he has been around for far longer than 250 years. In 1764 the antiquarian Dr Stukeley announced that the giant was a depiction of Hercules, a legendary hero who, like the giant, was depicted brandishing a club. However, it is equally plausible (or not, depending on your point of view) that there was a pagan inspiration behind the cutting of such a blatantly sexual figure, as shown by the fertility themes in the surviving folklore, and so the 200-foot (60.8-metre) giant may be the relic of a phallic cult. On the hill above his head is a small earthwork of bank and ditch called the Trendle or Frying Pan (not visible in the photograph), where a maypole used to be erected every year for May Day festivities. The maypole, as well as symbolizing a tree, is a phallic symbol, and the dancing and other activities which used to take place nationwide on May Day were directed towards the encouragement of fertility in man, beast and the whole of nature. The giant himself was once considered a source of fertility: women would sit on the figure in hope of bearing a child; unmarried girls would pray at his feet for the gift of a husband; and married couples would have intercourse on the figure to ensure pregnancy.

Chysauster Prehistoric Village, Cornwall
Well-preserved prehistoric settlements are not particularly common, but in a small area of Cornwall two of the best are to be found: Carn Euny (see p. 32) and Chysauster, shown here. Nine small houses survive, each with a courtyard from which tiny rooms lead off. The main room of the house has a flat stone in the ground with a socket hole, which presumably held a wooden post supporting a thatched roof. Covered drains, open hearths and stone basins for grinding grain can also be found, and the houses all had terraced gardens. Workrooms have been identified, and animal sheds, and as at Carn Euny there was an underground chamber or fogou here, though it is not so well preserved.

Cissbury Ring Hillfort, West Sussex

The hill which is now crowned by Cissbury Ring hillfort was said to have originally been a lump of earth thrown off the Devil's spade as he dug out the Devil's Dyke, north of Brighton. The Devil's superhuman powers apart, the Iron Age hillfort is yet another example, among many, of what could be achieved by sheer strength and determination using basic tools. It has been calculated that the ramparts comprised 60,000 tons of chalk, and were protected by a wall of 8,000–12,000 tree trunks at least 15 feet (4.5 metres) long. Although the wood has long since decayed, the ramparts are still impressive and enclose an area of 65 acres (26 hectares). The defensive nature of the fort is illustrated by the discovery of a hoard of over 400 beach pebbles intended for use as sling-stones, though the fort had been abandoned by the time the Romans invaded England.

Numerous overgrown hollows in the west side of the fort are evidence of the hill's early industrial history, because in Neolithic times, around 3,000 years before the hillfort was constructed, flint mining had taken place there. About 250 blocked mine shafts have been discovered: the mines were around 40 feet (12 metres) deep, with galleries leading off. Finds include picks made from the antlers of red deer, shovels made from animals' shoulder blades and a miner's lamp carved from a lump of chalk.

Perhaps it was the existence of the mines which led to the development of the belief that an underground passage led from the fort to the now-demolished Offington Hall, 2 miles (3.2 kilometres) away.

Cley Hill Hillfort, Wiltshire

Lying between Frome and Warminster, Cley Hill's summit was in the Iron Age sculpted into a fortress, the single bank and ditch still being visible, though the later chalk quarry seems to have destroyed the fort's entrance.

Evidence of the occupation of this hilltop site can be found in the hollows on the north-west, which show where huts were sited. There are also two round barrows on the hilltop. Warminster, just down the road, was famous in the 1960s as the UFO capital of England.

Cley Hill Hillfort,
Wiltshire

Creswell Crags, Derbyshire

At first glance, this wooded limestone gorge appears to be simply an impressive geographical feature which has been spoiled by the intrusion of a modern road. But Creswell Crags conceals something that takes us back way beyond the times of the peoples who left the relics illustrated in the rest of this book, and, in fact, makes them look almost contemporary with ourselves. In the gorge can be seen twenty caves which were home to our early ancestors of 30,000 years ago. Using flint tools, they hunted the mammoth, bison, reindeer and woolly rhinoceros which also lived here. More recently, a mere 13,000 years ago, after the caves had been unoccupied for a long period, they became home to a more modern kind of man. Today the caves are kept closed, but can be viewed through grilles, and a trail leads past the more important caves, with names such as Boat House Cave, Church Hole Cave, Pin Hole Cave, Robin Hood's Cave and Mother Grundy's Parlour.

Croft Ambrey Hillfort, Hereford & Worcester

Croft Ambrey hillfort has been carefully excavated, so that all seven phases of its construction have been identified. The hill was first occupied around 550 BC, when a small enclosure was protected by a rampart and ditch. In successive centuries bigger fortifications were built, enclosing a larger area, and periodically the gateway was redesigned and strengthened.

A sacred site was one of the many discoveries uncovered during archaeological excavations, at first in the form of a level terrace cut into the hillside, but later covered by a mound up to 5 feet (1.5 metres) high. Whatever religious ceremonies were performed here left behind broken pottery, charcoal, ash and burned bone.

The Devil's Arrows, North Yorkshire

Three huge standing stones (only two are visible here) form an alignment known as the Devil's Arrows – a fourth stone was pulled down in the sixteenth century by vandals in search of treasure. They range from 18 to 22 feet (5.5 to 6.8 metres) tall. The stones take their name from a story told to explain their presence here. The Devil was out to destroy the Christian settlement at Aldborough and fired four 'arrows' from Howe Hill near Fountains Abbey, but his aim was poor and the missiles fell short. The stones do indeed appear to have come from some distance away, the millstone grit from which they are formed being found at Knaresborough $6\frac{1}{2}$ miles (10.5 kilometres) away, and somehow, with great difficulty, they must have been transported from there. Why this should have been done is not clear, but in past centuries the St Barnabas Fair was held in a field close to the arrows, and antiquarian William Stukeley has suggested that the fair may have been the successor to ceremonies held at the Devil's Arrows themselves in even earlier times.

Dorset Cursus, near Cranbourne, Dorset

Dorset is one of England's richest counties in terms of visible prehistoric sites. It is particularly rich in round barrows and tumuli – Bronze Age burial mounds. This selection on the downs near Cranbourne shows a variety of shapes: take your pick from the possible barrow types which describe their shape – bowl, bell, disc, saucer and pond. Also in this area is an important Neolithic monument, in fact it is one of the largest prehistoric monuments in Britain, though visually it is now insignificant if you don't know what you are looking for. This is the so-called Dorset Cursus, two parallel banks running for 6 miles (9.6 kilometres) from Bokerley Down to Thickthorn Down, and now best seen on Bottlebush Down. There are long barrows closely linked to it, so maybe the Cursus was something to do with a Neolithic cult of the dead. No one, however, knows for certain.

Eggardon Hillfort, Dorset
The Iron Age hillfort on Eggardon Hill is very impressive, with three ramparts and ditches circling the hilltop and enclosing an area of 20 acres (8 hectares). There is evidence of a landslip in one section of the ramparts after the fort was built, and new fortifications had to be quickly constructed further down the hill. The people who built and presumably lived in this fortified settlement didn't leave many traces behind them, except for around 500 hollows in the ground which seem to have been storage pits. A few have been excavated, and flint knives and scrapers were found, but nothing else. Such tantalizing remains raise more questions than they answer, such as why were so many storage pits needed? What did the inhabitants keep in them? And why were flint tools left in the pits? Will the remains of our twentieth-century lifestyle be so enigmatic?

Figsbury Rings Hillfort, Wiltshire

Figsbury Rings is, in most respects, a typical Wiltshire hillfort – except for the unusual inner ditch. This appears to be unfinished: was it dug out while the hillfort was in use, for some unknown purpose, or was it delineating an enclosure that was in existence before the hillfort proper was built, a causewayed camp or meeting place in Neolithic times?

Grimes Graves, Norfolk

This bumpy landscape in Norfolk is reminiscent of the patterns left in seaside mud or sand by the retreating tide, but in this case it's caused by human activity. Grimes Graves (Grim is the Devil) is an early industrial site, where flint was quarried as long as 5,000 years ago. The hollows are the remains of hundreds of filled-in mine shafts. In some areas the flint was mined from shallow surface pits; in others 39-foot (12-metre) shafts were sunk. One of these deeper shafts is open to the public, access being by means of an iron ladder.

The miners chipped away at the flint using picks made from the antlers of red deer, and they worked along passages and galleries radiating out from the main shaft. The flint was hauled up to the surface in baskets. In one mine, which apparently produced poor quality flint, the miners left objects which seem to have been intended to work magic. They were a crude chalk statuette of a pregnant woman, which was placed on a ledge, and in front of it were a phallus made of chalk and a pile of flints and antler picks. Clearly the message to the god or goddess was: please make our mines fertile!

Grimspound Settlement, Devon

As with the name of Grimes Graves in Norfolk (see opposite) the name of Grimspound in Devon also refers to Grim, the Devil. The location of this cattle farmers' enclosure suggests that Dartmoor in the Bronze Age, around 3,000 years ago, was not as inhospitable as it often is today. All that survives of the prehistoric cattle ranch is a stone wall enclosing 4 acres (1.6 hectares), inside which are heaps of stones marking the remains of dwelling huts with hearths, store huts and cattle pens.

Hambledon Hill Hillfort, Dorset

The hillfort on Hambledon Hill rivals that other major Iron Age hillfort in Dorset, Maiden Castle (see p. 70), while close by is another impressive hillfort on Hod Hill (see p. 60). The summit of Hambledon Hill is completely enclosed by banks and ditches which wind sinuously along its flanks, enclosing an area of over 24 acres (10 hectares). Before these were dug during the Iron Age, the hill had been the site of a Neolithic causewayed camp, and there is still a Neolithic long barrow 230 feet (70 metres) long and 6 feet (1.8 metres) high inside the hillfort. Over 200 hollows inside the fort probably indicate the site of huts.

Hembury Castle, Devon

The first signs of occupation here date back around 6,000 years, when an earthwork of the type now known as a causewayed camp was constructed, occupying the southern end of the hill. In addition to ditches and ramparts, wooden post holes were found, and evidence of domestic occupation in the form of hearths, cooking pots, flint scrapers, querns for grinding grain, and the remains of food such as grain and hazelnuts, which had been stored in shallow pits. However, the causewayed camp may not have been a permanent settlement for a whole community. The finds show that someone lived there – perhaps the farmer who grew the wheat and barley whose remains were found in the storage pits – but it is thought that causewayed camps were places where the people of the area would meet at certain times of the year to perform seasonal rituals.

Much later, 'only' 2,000 years ago, in the Iron Age, the hill was reoccupied and a larger fortress constructed, the banks and ditches of which are still clearly defined, despite the extensive tree cover on the hill today.

*Herefordshire Beacon
Hillfort, Hereford &
Worcester*

This is without doubt one of the
most impressive Iron Age hillforts
in Britain. Its banks and ditches can
still be clearly seen as they follow
the 1,000-foot contour of the
Malvern Hills, enclosing 32 acres
(13 hectares) of the hilltops.
Originally only a quarter the
size, the hillfort was much enlarged
later in the Iron Age. Ramparts are
usually defensive structures, and a
considerable amount of effort would
have been needed to build them –
but it is hard to see how an area the
size and shape of this hillfort could
have been easily defended against
invaders. Perhaps the ramparts
were symbolic defences, marking
territorial boundaries.

Hod Hill Hillfort, Dorset

One of numerous fine hillforts in Dorset, its ramparts being built and altered in several phases during the Iron Age. Later reinforcements may have been triggered by the invasion of the Romans, which took place in the year AD 43; but all in vain, because Hod Hill was one of the largest of twenty hillforts to fall to Vespasian (emperor of Rome, AD 69–79). The fort was occupied at the time, and the circular shapes of hundreds of huts have been identified by archaeologists. But one hut was set apart from the others, in a rectangular enclosure, and it seems that this may have been the chieftain's hut, because the Romans concentrated their attack upon it. Eleven iron ballista bolts (a ballista was a machine for firing missiles) were found on the site of this hut, and it is feasible that when the Romans destroyed the chieftain's hut, the fortress surrendered. The Romans took over the hilltop, destroyed the surviving dwellings, and constructed their own fortress in the north-west corner. Its banks can be seen in the photograph. The Roman fort probably accommodated around 850 soldiers, but their occupation only lasted a few years until AD 51, when the buildings were destroyed by fire.

The Hurlers Stone Circles, Cornwall

Three stone circles close together is an unexpected find, but here on Bodmin Moor in Cornwall are the remains of The Hurlers, three circles in a line. Unfortunately many of the stones are missing, but enough remain to show that they appear to have been carefully erected, so that all the stones seem to be the same height. According to folklore, they were men turned to stone for playing at hurling the ball on the Sabbath. It was also said that it was difficult to count the number of stones, a problem overcome by the ingenious man who (allegedly) placed a loaf on each stone and then subtracted the number of loaves left at the end from the number he started with, the answer being the number of stones.

Knowlton Circles, Dorset
These circles originally comprised several circular enclosures defined by banks and ditches, but today only one, the Central Circle, survives. It was probably a henge monument: a Neolithic sacred enclosure where unknown rites and ceremonies were performed. Inside the circle is a ruined twelfth-century church with a fifteenth-century tower, showing how the sacred sites of prehistory retained their sanctity and were sometimes reused for later religious purposes. Other examples of this include prehistoric standing stones that survive in churchyards, or churchyards which are circular in shape. East of the Central Circle is the Great Barrow, a burial mound still standing 20 feet (6 metres) high, seen in the right background of the photograph. Other barrows existed, but are now lost due to ploughing.

Lambourn Seven Barrows, Berkshire

This is the place to see not only a good collection of round barrows, but also bell barrows, bowl barrows, disc barrows and saucer barrows. These names distinguish the different shaped burial mounds, which date from the Bronze Age. From the remains found inside them it seems that men were buried in bell barrows and women in disc barrows. The groups of barrows here in ancient Wessex may have formed a graveyard for the aristocrats of the time. Artefacts such as bronze awls (a pointed tool for piercing wood and leather), bronze knives, a pygmy cup and a small jet amulet were found with cremation burials in the barrows.

Lanyon Quoit, Cornwall

Several 'quoits' can be found in the most south-westerly part of Cornwall, and Lanyon Quoit shown here is the most accessible. A quoit (or cromlech or dolmen) consists of a large capstone (in this case weighing 13.4 tons) supported on several smaller upright stones, the whole forming a burial chamber which would once have been covered by earth. There are still traces of the earth mound at Lanyon, visible to the trained eye, but this site in not wholly authentic because in 1815 it collapsed in a storm and some of the stones were damaged. Several years later it was re-erected, but on a smaller scale and the wrong way round.

Long Man of Wilmington, East Sussex

There are two human figures cut into the chalk of southern England: the Cerne Abbas Giant of Dorset (see p. 35) and the Long Man of Wilmington in East Sussex. They are very different in appearance, though both are enigmatic, in purpose and in dating. The Long Man is about 230 feet (70 metres) tall and holds two staffs, though they were probably originally something else, perhaps a rake and scythe, or spears, or the gates of heaven, depending on which identification of the Long Man you prefer: St Paul, Mohammed, King Harold, a Roman soldier, Mercury, a Saxon haymaker, Baldur the Beautiful, Apollo, Thor, Woden, Beowulf, a surveyor ... the list is endless. Unfortunately the true appearance of the original Long Man is now unknown, since he was 'restored' in the 1870s. The most colourful explanation for the figure's presence on the Sussex Downs is that he was a giant who died or was killed on the hill and was outlined where he lay.

Long Meg and Her Daughters Stone Circle, Cumbria

Long Meg and Her Daughters often becomes one of the favourite stone circles of people who visit it. Much less visited than the more famous Cumbrian circle of Castlerigg (see p. 34), this is just as impressive in its own way. One of the largest in Britain, the oval 'circle' of fifty-nine stones, twenty-seven still standing (there were originally about seventy stones), measures about 360 feet (100 metres) by 305 feet (93 metres). The stones of the circle are the daughters, and Long Meg herself is a 12-foot (3.6-metre) standing stone just outside the circle – at the bottom of the photograph. It is possible that Long Meg was here first, and the circle was purposely set up close to her. There are carvings of rings and spirals on the stone, which may reflect the movement of the sun towards midsummer and back towards midwinter.

According to tradition, Long Meg and Her Daughters were a coven of witches who fell under the spell of Michael Scot, a wizard, and were turned to stone. The stones are said to be uncountable, and if anyone can count them twice and arrive at the same total, the spell will be broken. When an attempt was made in the eighteenth century to destroy the circle by blasting, a thunderstorm broke out which caused the destroyers to stop work.

Mam Tor Hillfort, Derbyshire

Known locally as Shivering Mountain, because of the landslides which regularly occur, Mam Tor carries on its summit the remains of Derbyshire's largest hillfort, covering 16 acres (7 hectares). The outer banks and ditches are still clearly defined, and excavations inside the fort have produced post-holes, hearths and pottery showing that the place was occupied at some stage. The people of 3,000 or so years ago must have been remarkably tough: 1,700 feet (517 metres) up on an exposed hillside would not seem to be the most pleasant place to set up home, especially in the winter – unless the climate was different then, which it may well have been.

Maiden Castle, Dorset
If you could only visit one hillfort in Britain, Maiden Castle should undoubtedly be your choice. It is not simply its size (45 acres/ 18 hectares in area and 1.5 miles/ 2.5 kilometres around the inner circumference), though that is impressive enough; it is the sheer magnificence of the total structure, with its steep banks and deep ditches, and the complexity of its entrance earthworks (seen in left foreground). The fort grew and evolved over time, starting around 3000 BC, until eventually it contained a large and strongly defended Iron Age town. Then, in AD 43, the Romans came, and Maiden Castle fell to an army led by Vespasian. The war cemetery resulting from this encounter has been uncovered just outside the eastern gateway, and in Dorchester Museum you can see the spine of one of the defenders with a Roman iron arrowhead embedded in the bones.

After the defeat, people continued to live in the fort for a few years. It was only some twenty years later it was abandoned and replaced by the modern town of Dorchester nearby. However, in the late fourth century AD a Romano-Celtic temple with adjoining house was built inside the fort. The foundations for these buildings can still be seen in the north-east sector.

Men-an-Tol, Cornwall

Like Lanyon Quoit (see p. 65) not far away, the Men-an-Tol has been 'interfered with'. No one now knows the original layout of this Cornish site, or even what sort of monument it was. It is likely to have been a burial chamber, but it could have been a stone circle. The Men-an-Tol is the holed stone (the name simply means 'stone with a hole'), and it could have been the entrance stone to a burial chamber. Whatever its original purpose, it later became the focus of healing rituals. Naked children were passed three times through the hole and then drawn along the grass three times in an easterly direction. This was thought to cure scrofula (a form of tuberculosis) and rickets. Adults seeking relief from rheumatism, spine troubles or ague were advised to crawl through the hole nine times against the sun. The repeated crawling through the stone could have symbolized rebirth. The stone was also believed to have powers of prophecy. Nineteenth-century folklorist Robert Hunt said that 'if two brass pins are carefully laid across each other on the top edge of the stone, any question put to the rock will be answered by the pins acquiring, through some unknown agency, a peculiar motion'. A pity that he doesn't also say how you should interpret this 'peculiar motion'!

**_Merrivale Hut Circles,
Devon_**
Some of Dartmoor's many
prehistoric sites are not easily
accessible, being distant from
a road. Little effort, however, is
required to explore the variety
of remains at Merrivale, since they
straddle a main road. Dating from
the Bronze Age, the structures
include hut circles (as shown in
the photograph), barrows, cairns,
a stone circle and three stone rows.
Clearly this was a ritual landscape,
and probably the rituals centred
on death, but beyond that all is lost
in the mists of time.

The Merry Maidens Stone Circle, Cornwall

This neat little stone circle, tucked away in a typically Cornish land-scape, has the intriguing name of The Merry Maidens. This originates in the folklore belief that the stones were once a group of young girls who misbehaved by dancing on a Sunday, to the music of two pipers, and they were all turned to stone as a punishment. The Pipers are two tall (over 4 metres) standing stones in a field not far away.

Normanton Down Barrow Cemetery, Wiltshire

Not far from Stonehenge is the Normanton Down barrow cemetery, a fine collection of burial mounds where, just as at the Winterbourne Stoke cemetery (see p. 101), it is probable that important figures were buried. There are two dozen barrows from the Neolithic and Bronze Ages spread out across the downs, in varying designs and sizes, and the objects that have been discovered inside them include, in addition to skeletons and cremation burials, bronze daggers, shields and axes, a ceremonial mace, beads and pendants of amber, urns and cups, and a considerable quantity of gold items, reinforcing the idea that this was a mausoleum for the Bronze Age equivalent of royalty.

Old Oswestry Hillfort, Shropshire

Old Oswestry Iron Age hillfort stands on the edge of the town of Oswestry, and its name suggests that the first settlement was located inside the fortress. The low winter light accentuates the complex construction of this magnificent hillfort, which took shape in several phases. The purpose of the lines of hollows on either side of the long entrance passage is not known, but they may have somehow helped in the protection of the potentially vulnerable entrance. Old Oswestry's traditional name was Caer Ogyrfan, the fort of Gogyrfan, who was the father of Guinevere, King Arthur's wife; but this Arthurian connection unfortunately exists only in folklore.

Pilsdon Pen, Dorset

There are several fine hillforts in Dorset, and Pilsdon Pen is one of the finest, the hilltop still encircled by deep ditches and steep ramparts. Hut sites dating from the Iron Age have been discovered during archaeological excavations, and one of the huts seems to have been used as a goldsmith's workshop. This was deduced from the discovery of a crucible with beads of gold still attached to it. The huts were replaced by a large rectangular wooden building, but no clues to its purpose were found. Perhaps it was used for religious or ceremonial purposes. Hillforts were not simply fortified stockades where people took refuge in times of tribal warfare, but seem to have acted as settlements where all aspects of life were carried on, as shown by the presence of a goldsmith's workshop. Unless the ramparts are now overgrown by trees, hillforts today are usually good places to go walking (if public access is allowed) because of the magnificent views they offer over the surrounding countryside.

Rollright Stones,
Oxfordshire
Like a necklet of shark's teeth, from
the air the Rollright Stones seem
to form a barricade against the
advancing trees. Also known as
the King's Men, this stone circle
on the Oxfordshire/Warwickshire
border is close to two other Bronze
Age sites, the Whispering Knights
and the King Stone, and together
the three sites feature in a folktale
which gave them their strange
names.

Once upon a time all the stones were human beings, a king and his army. They were marching through the area when they were met by a witch who said to the king:

Seven long strides shalt thou take.
If Long Compton thou canst see
King of England thou shalt be.
The king's reply was:
Stick, stock, stone,
As King of England I shall be known.
But after he had strode forward seven times, he found that his view of the village in the valley was blocked by an earth mound known as the Archdruid's Barrow.
The witch then decreed:
As Long Compton thou canst not see,
King of England thou shalt not be.
Rise up stick, and stand still stone,
For King of England thou shalt be none.
Thou and thy men hoar stones shall be
And myself an eldern tree.

The name of the Whispering Knights (left) is appropriate: standing close together in a field just along the road from the stone circle, the five stones that once formed a burial chamber do now resemble a group of knights huddled together whispering conspiratorially. In a field across the road from the King's Men, the King's Stone stands alone, 8 feet (2.5 metres) tall (see facing page). Nearby can be discerned the remains of a mound, now reduced by ploughing: this was the fateful Archdruid's Barrow.

The stones have also been the subject of other folklore beliefs: the King's Men were said to be uncountable, and attempts to move the stones have ended in disaster. Pieces were chipped off the King Stone as good luck charms, and once a year the local youngsters would meet beside it to dance, eat cakes and drink ale. Midsummer's Eve was an especially potent time, and people would traditionally form a circle around the King's Stone. It was said that the stone (the king) would go to a nearby spring for a drink when the clock struck midnight.

The Rollright Stones have retained their connection with witchcraft, hinted at in the folktale. The witch turned herself into an elder tree, and it was believed that if this tree were cut, it (she) would bleed. Modern-day witches still use the stones as a place to perform their rites, or so it is said. In the late 1970s a scientific project took place here. Known as the Dragon Project, its intention was to explore the possibility that ancient sites are the focus of unusual energies, and to this end monitoring of the Rollright sites was carried out over several years, using ultrasonic detection, electric field detection, microwave and Geiger monitoring, infra-red photography, dowsing and clairvoyance. Various anomalies were detected, the significance of which are still being assessed.

The Sanctuary, Wiltshire
The name of this site, 'The Sanctuary', only dates from the seventeenth century, and so may be a bit misleading. Today only post-hole indicators survive, marked out by archaeologists after they discovered that successive circular wooden (later incorporating stone) buildings stood here, starting around 3000 BC. The Sanctuary was linked to Avebury henge (see p. 18) 1.5 miles (2.4 kilometres) away by an avenue of standing stones, and so presumably had something to do with whatever rituals were performed at Avebury. Large numbers of human bones were found in the soil at The Sanctuary, together with evidence of feasting, and so it is probable that death rituals were performed there, perhaps involving the laying out of corpses until they rotted or were eaten by animals, after which the bones were gathered and placed in tombs or ritually scattered.

Today, the Sanctuary is not an atmospheric place. This is guaranteed by its close proximity to a main road.

Silbury Hill, Wiltshire
Silbury Hill looks even larger from the road than it does from the air: 130 feet (40 metres) high, it's the largest man-made prehistoric mound in Europe. A site of major importance, it's also very close to at least two other major sites: Avebury henge (see p. 18) and West Kennet long barrow (see p. 98). Its very presence is a huge question mark on this Wiltshire landscape, the question being: why was it built?

Despite serious archaeological excavations, no one has yet found any trace of a corpse or tomb inside it, and so there are doubts about it being a burial mound. Silbury was built in three stages starting around 2700 BC, and it's clear that several million man-hours must have been clocked up for some other reason than merely to keep the natives occupied. Perhaps folklore is right after all: according to legend, King Sil is inside, in a golden coffin, or on horseback and dressed in golden armour. Another suggestion is that Silbury can be used as a giant sun-dial, if a pole is stuck into the top; or maybe it is the pregnant Earth Mother, squatting to give birth. (See Michael Dames's book, *The Silbury Treasure*.)

South Cadbury Castle, Somerset

King Arthur's castle of Camelot may have been here in the fifth century AD, inside the hillfort of South Cadbury in Somerset. But it was by no means the earliest use of the hill as a settlement. There is evidence that people first lived on the hill during the eighth century BC, and over the centuries following, each generation built new fortifications and timber buildings. So that today, although the buildings have all long disappeared, the outer ramparts encircling the top of the hill are still impressive. Archaeological finds such as buried animals which had been sacrificed, suggest that shrines and temples were built here, and even after the Romans moved in around AD 70 or 80, there may have been a temple on the hill. The Arthurian occupation (if indeed South Cadbury really was Camelot) lasted for about two generations around AD 470. The great king's presence has left folklore memories, such as the belief that King Arthur and his knights lie sleeping inside the hill, waiting for the call to come to England's aid. Every seven years, Arthur leads his men out on Midsummer's Eve, and they go to a spring by the church at Sutton Montis for water.

Stanton Drew, Somerset

Hidden away in north-east Somerset, close to the village of Stanton Drew, are the remains of a potentially important Neolithic site. It comprises three stone circles, avenues of stones leading towards the River Chew, a standing stone known as Hautville's Quoit and a stone structure called The Cove. Most of the remains are on private land, but The Cove can be seen from the churchyard. The small photograph shows one of the smaller stone circles and, to the left, a segment of the so-called Great Circle. Insignificant from the air, and almost lost in the agricultural landscape, this important complex – which may in fact rival Stonehenge and Avebury in importance – was laid out with huge blocks of stone.

Folklore records that these stones are a petrified (in the literal sense) wedding party. The Cove is the parson, bride and bridegroom, while the circles are the dancing wedding guests. Another small group of stones (possibly those in the photograph, between the large and small circles) are the musicians. The fiddler refused to play after midnight, so the dancers were delighted when a stranger dressed in black appeared and started to play for them. He played faster and faster, and the dancers couldn't stop. Only at dawn did the music stop, and by that time the dancers had been turned to stone. The fiddler, who was of course the Devil, said he would come back one day to play for them again – but they are still waiting. It was also believed that the stones were impossible to count. In 1750 John Wood wrote: 'No one, say the country people about Stantondrue, was ever able to reckon the number of these metamorphosed stones, or to take a draught of them, though several have attempted to do both, and proceeded till they were either struck dead upon the spot, or with such an illness as soon carried them off.' When Wood himself tried to count the stones, a cloudburst followed, and the villagers were sure that the one was caused by the other.

Stonehenge, Wiltshire

Stonehenge must be Britain's best-known prehistoric monument – though it is also true to say that when visited it rarely lives up to people's expectations, as it seems much smaller than they had imagined. Unfortunately it has been very unsympathetically treated in the past, with the result that it is overshadowed by ugly reminders of the twentieth century: noisy roads, high fences, a huge car park, lots of concrete. There are plans afoot to change all this, and it is to be hoped that Stonehenge will eventually regain its silent domination of Salisbury Plain.

It is a complex structure, having gradually developed over a long period of time, and it does not stand alone: the countryside all around is littered with prehistoric sites, some of them with purposes still unknown, such as the linear earthwork known as the Cursus, and hundreds of burial mounds where the royalty of the time were probably buried. Stonehenge vastly predates the Druids, who are erroneously linked with it in the popular mind. In fact they came to Britain around 2,000 years after it had been finished!

The current belief is that Stonehenge was some kind of astronomical structure, with stones marking the midsummer and midwinter sunrises and sunsets. This may have been just one of its functions – and its appearance and significance probably changed with each new generation. There is no doubting its major importance, which is shown by the fact that some of the stones were brought vast distances. The smaller bluestones probably came from the Preseli Hills in South Wales, while the larger stones are thought to have come from the Marlborough

Downs a few miles away. Folklore suggests that all the stones came from Africa via Ireland, where they were set up by a race of giants who used their healing properties. Then they were known as the Giant's Dance, and were later moved by the wizard Merlin to the present site, at the request of King Aurelius. Even today in the supposedly rational twentieth century many people seem to almost worship Stonehenge, with modern Druids, pagans, and New Age followers vying to claim the stones for themselves, necessitating a huge police presence at significant times of the year. Despite all this, Stonehenge retains its dignity - and its mystery.

Stoney Littleton Long Barrow, near Bath

The stone chamber into which burials were placed inside Stoney Littleton long barrow extends 48 feet (14.4 metres) into the earth mound which covers it. The passage is only 4 feet (1.2 metres) high in places, and small stone chambers open off it.

Although it was clearly in use as a burial site for a long period of time around 5,000 years ago, as with other Neolithic long barrows nothing is definitely known about the beliefs of the people whose sacred site this was. There are, however, some intriguing possibilities. A large fossil ammonite on a stone is prominently sited at the main entrance, with another at the entrance to one of the interior chambers. Dr G. T. Meaden felt that spiral shells and fossils were signs of the goddess, and described in his book *The Goddess of the Stones* how the passage at Stoney Littleton was aligned to correspond with the rising sun on midwinter's day, thus suggesting that the barrow was not only a tomb but a temple. He wrote, it was built as the 'womb-tomb of the Great Goddess who awaited the annual return of the sun'.

Swinside Stone Circle, Cumbria

This fine stone circle has fifty-five stones still standing, the tallest 7 feet 6 inches (2.3 metres) high. Cumbria has a trio of impressive stone circles, the others being Castlerigg (see p. 34) and Long Meg and Her Daughters (see p. 67). The stones at Swinside are said to be countless, and an alternative name for them was Sunken Kirk, from the belief that at this place the Devil nightly pulled down a church that was being built during the day.

Uffington Castle, Oxfordshire

This Iron Age hillfort is situated immediately above the chalk figure of the Uffington White Horse (in the larger photograph he would be located just off to the bottom left). In the space between the horse and the fort are two oval mounds, one of which, when excavated in 1857, was found to contain almost fifty Roman skeletons. Five of them had coins placed between their teeth, to pay the ferryman to take them across the River Styx into the underworld.

The earliest rampart of the fort consisted of two lines of posts with chalk rubble packed in between them. Down the years, numerous breaks have been made in the ramparts, but the main entrance was at the west, clearly seen on the right-hand side of the photograph. Stretching from side to side of the photograph, beyond the hillfort, is the Ridgeway, an ancient track which passes numerous prehistoric sites as it runs along the edge of the downs.

Uffington White Horse, Oxfordshire

The chalk figure cut into a hill at Uffington is identified as a horse, but his reason for being there is not at all clear. Folklore has turned him into a dragon, and identified a flat-topped hill below him as Dragon Hill. This is meant to be the place where St George slew the dragon – as proved by the fact that the top of the hill is bare of grass because the dragon's blood was spilled there.

Recent scientific dating methods show the figure to have been originally cut in the late Bronze Age – over 3,000 years ago – but he has been repaired and tidied up many times since then. In the past he was 'scoured' every seven years, this event being accompanied by assorted festivities and no doubt a lot of drinking. Was he perhaps a tribal emblem? This was clearly an important place, as the hillfort now known as Uffington Castle is just

above his head (see p. 94), and the prehistoric track, the Ridgeway, is also not far away. An intriguing point is that the Uffington White Horse (as he is usually called) can only be properly seen from the air. You can walk along the hilltop and stand above his head, but you don't get any proper idea of what he looks like unless, like Jason Hawkes, you take to the air and fly over him.

Wayland's Smithy, Oxfordshire

Hidden away in a small wood, Wayland's Smithy takes its name (since the tenth century AD) from a folk belief that it was here that Wayland the Smith, a Saxon god, worked, and that if a traveller's horse lost a shoe, he should leave the animal here with a coin on one of the stones. On his return he would find the money gone and his horse newly shod.

In fact the structure is a Neolithic long barrow dating back more than 5,000 years, and predating the Saxons by 4,000 years. The present structure is an earth mound 196 feet (60 metres) long, which in fact overlies an earlier, smaller barrow. At its widest end is a stone burial chamber, at the entrance to which are four upright stones 10 feet (3 metres) high. It is these stones which can be seen in the photograph.

Wayland's Smithy is close to the prehistoric trackway known as the Ridgeway, and only a mile away are Uffington Castle and Uffington White Horse (see pp 94 and 96).

West Kennet Avenue, Wiltshire

One of the features of the spectacular Neolithic landscape around Avebury in Wiltshire is the West Kennet Avenue, which once consisted of 100 pairs of stones standing approximately 50 feet (15 metres) apart. They stretched for 1^1/2 miles (2.5 kilometres) between the southern entrance of Avebury and The Sanctuary (see pp 18 and 82).

The stones are around 10 feet (3 metres) tall, and alternate in shape between tall narrow ones (male?) and broad lozenge shapes (female?). Only the northern third of the avenue has been restored, leading to Avebury, some of the stones of which can be seen top right. It is assumed that the Avenue was a processional way, used during the performance of religious rituals, but any further suggestions would be pure speculation.

West Kennet Long Barrow, Wiltshire

The impressive Neolithic tomb known as West Kennet long barrow is another of the fine prehistoric sites in this area of Wiltshire. Within sight is Silbury Hill, while not much further away is Avebury with its major henge monument (see pp 18 and 82).

The photograph clearly shows the huge size of this burial chamber: the earth mound is more than 320 feet (100 metres) long and 8 feet (2.4 metres) high. The stone-built burial chamber is behind the row of large standing stones, and it extends about 33 feet (10 metres) into the mound. It is possible to enter the chamber: the roof is about 7.5 feet (2.3 metres) high. In past centuries, before careful archaeological excavation could be undertaken, the tomb was damaged by people searching for whatever they could find; and in 1685 a Dr Toope of Marlborough dug up human bones in order to make 'noble medicine' with which to treat his patients. Nevertheless, forty-six burials have been found, and it is thought that the tomb was in use for as long as 1,000 years. After the last burial, the chamber was filled up with earth and stones, among which were found pieces of pottery, bone tools and beads, and then the chamber was sealed with huge stones. It was said that at sunrise on Midsummer Day, the barrow was visited by a ghostly priest with a large white hound.

Windmill Hill Causewayed Camp, Wiltshire

Windmill Hill is close to Avebury henge (see p. 18) and is today rather featureless, but it is the site of an important Neolithic meeting place known as a causewayed camp. It is the largest known causewayed camp in Britain, covering around 21 acres (9 hectares), and three concentric rings of ditches were dug around the hill. When the camp was excavated in the 1920s and later, over 1,000 pottery vessels were found, and many animal bones, including complete skeletons of a young pig, a dog, and a young sheep or goat. These were probably buried as sacrifices or offerings. The other bones, including those of cattle, pigs, sheep, deer, horses and hares, suggest ritual feasting. Human bones were also found, some from children buried deliberately, and some possibly from corpses which had been left exposed until the flesh had rotted away before the bones were scattered in rituals. Seventy human skulls were found together, possibly marking an area devoted to death.

The finding of small carved chalk objects possibly representing female figures and phalluses suggests that at least some of the rituals held here were to promote fertility. But the discovery of other objects such as flint tools, axes and pottery suggests that the camp also acted as a market where people came to exchange goods, including some which were perishable and have not survived. Today the only visible relics on the hill are Bronze Age burial mounds on the summit. The hill came into use as a cemetery long after the causewayed camp had been abandoned.

Winterbourne Stoke Barrow Cemetery, Wiltshire

In Wiltshire and Dorset especially, there are some fine collections of prehistoric barrows (earthen burial chambers), but the most accessible by foot is the so-called barrow cemetery near Winterbourne Stoke. There is a Neolithic long barrow (over 5,000 years old) close to the road junction, then a whole collection of later Bronze Age barrows (about 2,500 years old) are visible to the north-east. The names of the barrows vary according to their design; for example, the two in the left foreground are known as bell barrows, while the two behind them are disc barrows. To the right of them is a bowl barrow and then a saucer barrow, with another bowl barrow in front. When excavated, the two bell barrows were found to contain items such as a wooden box with bronze fittings containing a cremation, a tree-trunk coffin containing a skeleton, and several bronze daggers. The cemetery was in use over a long period of time, with some of the barrows being reused. Perhaps this was a royal cemetery where the most important people were buried.

Yarnbury Castle, Wiltshire
Yarnbury, a circular fort on low ground, was protected by triple banks and ditches, perhaps because it didn't benefit from a naturally defensive hilltop location. A faint circle inside the fort indicates the line of the first fort on this site. The curved banks which can be seen at the right foreground, outside the entrance, were built to protect the entrance, so that anyone entering would have to do so indirectly, thus making it difficult for a large force of men to storm the entrance. From the eighteenth century until 1916, a sheep fair was held annually inside the fort, and the sheep-pens have left marks inside the enclosure, to the east.

Yeavering Bell Hillfort, Northumberland
A single stone rampart encircles two hilltops to form this Iron Age hillfort, while at each end there is a small crescent-shaped annexe (partly visible at right of photograph) walled in by a smaller wall, for some unknown purpose. Small circles throughout the fort mark the sites of around 130 huts, which were timber-built: this was once a sizeable settlement. The problem that always recurs when trying to envisage a thriving settlement on a now bleak hilltop is: was the weather then like it is now? Most people now would not contemplate the thought of living in such a place! Have we simply become too soft, or was the climate friendlier then?

SCOTLAND

The richness and variety in the ancient sites of Scotland make it a fruitful place for the lover of antiquities, with all areas having something special to offer. Unfortunately, the best are also the most inaccessible. The outlying islands of Shetland, Orkney and the Western Isles are especially rich in prehistoric sites. Lewis has the remarkable site of Callanish, a cross-shaped formation of standing stones, as well as a well-preserved broch (stone tower). The Orkney isles have numerous chambered cairns and passage graves, the most spectacular being Maes Howe, one of the finest examples of prehistoric architecture and workmanship in north-west Europe. It doesn't look much from the outside, but seen from inside the 15-foot-square chamber the 4,500-year-old structure is awe-inspiring. Henges, stone circles and brochs can also be found on Orkney; and the famous settlement of Skara Brae, buried in a sandstorm around 3,000 years ago, is yet another unique piece of history. Shetland also has prehistoric settlements, and one of the finest surviving brochs, standing 40 feet high, on Mousa Island.

That list of irresistible places only covers the islands! Back on the mainland of Scotland are to be found numerous fine hillforts, more brochs, and another antiquity rarely found elsewhere (except in Cornwall), the souterrain, which is an underground passage whose purpose is unclear. There are several in Scotland, though largely roofless now. Fine stone tombs of all descriptions are abundant, as also are stone circles. As in Wales, the availability of stone has meant that a large number of prehistoric structures in the Highlands and Islands of Scotland have survived the ravages of time – and they have also been protected by their relative inaccessibility. Their isolation in a wild and mountainous landscape gives them a power that has often been lost by similar structures in England and

Dun Telve Broch, Highland

the lowland regions of Wales and Scotland, which often sit lost and forlorn in the midst of an agricultural landscape.

But now in the late twentieth century even isolated sites are coming under pressure from increased numbers of visitors, as more people have more leisure time, more money, and their own transport, with the result that all the major sites have been taken into official guardianship. In some respects this is beneficial: the sites are protected, excavated, tidied up and interpreted, so that the casual visitor can easily understand what he is looking at. But all these trappings of guardianship tend to rob a site of its mystery: fences, shorn grass and kiosks are counter-productive if you are seeking atmosphere! Thankfully, in Scotland there are still surviving prehistoric structures that need physical effort to be reached, where municipal man has not yet taken over, and a subtle link back through the years to our ancestors may be sensed.

Clava Cairns

Cairnholy Chambered Cairns, Dumfries and Galloway

Two chambered cairns high on a hillside above Wigtown Bay go by the name Cairnholy; the photograph shows the facade and forecourt of Cairnholy I. The mound behind is about 140 feet (43 metres) long, and the entrance into the burial chamber was between the two central upright stones. Ritual ceremonies connected with death and burial were probably performed in the forecourt, where evidence of fires has been found. The dead would have been cremated before their remains were placed in the tomb; pottery found inside dates the activity to the Late Neolithic and Early Bronze Age periods.

Clava Cairns, Highland

Close to Culloden battlefield is an unusual and impressive prehistoric site, Clava Cairns, where three round cairns of stones are encircled by standing stones. Stones bearing enigmatic cupmarks were positioned inside the cairns; their significance is unknown.

Two of the cairns are passage graves, including the one shown in the photograph, with a passage leading into the centre. (They would originally have been roofed.) The three cairns are in a line, and the two passages also align, the alignment pointing to a place on the horizon where the midwinter sunset would have been in prehistoric times. This is just another piece of evidence that astronomical observations had a part to play in the rituals performed at many prehistoric sites, though no one now knows their precise significance – whether it was purely symbolic or had some practical value. Such sites as Clava Cairns tantalize us: they seem to offer so many clues, yet the puzzle is impossible to solve.

Dun Beag Broch, Highland

Dun Beag is a fine example of a Hebridean broch, sited on a rocky knoll high above its surroundings on the Island of Skye. Scotland had the broch as well as the hillfort: it was a defensive tower with drystone walls, usually hollow and containing galleries. Dun Beag was probably in use during the first millennium BC and into the first millennium AD. The building's diameter was 36 feet (11 metres), and the walls were around 13 feet (4 metres) thick. Chambers opened off the central courtyard to either side of the entrance (which would have been closed with a wooden door), and the chamber to the right had a stairway leading to the upper floors. The courtyard would have been open to the sky, and may have been a safe refuge for the occupant's livestock in times of danger.

Dun Telve and Dun Troddan Brochs, Highland
Dun Telve on the floor of Glenelg in Highland is another broch like Dun Beag on Skye (see p. 109), and one of many in northern Scotland, though Dun Telve is one of the best preserved. Part of the wall still stands over 30 feet (10 metres) high, and the double wall construction can be seen in the photograph. Looking down on Dun Telve from a hillside terrace are the remains of another very similar broch, Dun Troddan.

Easter Aquhorthies
Recumbent Stone Circle,
Aberdeenshire
This is a fine example of a
recumbent stone circle, a type
of circle largely confined to
Aberdeenshire, where there are
many examples. Built of a very
attractive local granite stone,
Easter Aquhorthies stone circle is
particularly impressive, with a huge
recumbent stone 12 feet 6 inches
(3.8 metres) long, flanked
by uprights 7 feet 6 inches
(2.5 metres) tall. Exactly why these
stones were placed flat in these
circles in Aberdeenshire is not clear,
but research has shown that the
stones usually align on the major
southern moonset, so yet again
some ritual purpose linked with
astronomical observations
seems likely.

The Grey Cairns of Camster, Highland

The Grey Cairns of Camster are two restored Neolithic chambered cairns, one round and the other long, sitting a short distance apart in their stark Highland setting. Low passages lead inside the cairns to burial chambers – in fact the long cairn has two passages leading to two separate chambers, and it is very likely that two round cairns preceded the long cairn which was later built over them. When excavations were carried out in the nineteenth century, any burials in the long cairn were destroyed, but finds from the round cairn included burnt bones, pottery and flint tools, as well as the remains of several skeletons.

The Hill O'Many Stanes, Highland

The Hill O'Many Stanes is an appropriate name for this site, also known as Mid Clyth stone rows. In a rocky landscape, the significance of these small boulders seemingly scattered at random on a moorland slope could easily be missed. Around 200 stones are arranged in twenty-two apparently parallel rows, but originally there may have been over 600 stones here. The formation is slightly fan-shaped, with the stones set carefully upright, possibly around 4,000 years ago. Professor Alexander Thom believed that the site had an astronomical function, and that the stones could have formed a kind of grid or computer by means of which observations of the moon were plotted. A prehistoric lunar observatory?

Kilmartin Cairn Cemetery, Argyll and Bute

Kilmartin cairn cemetery consists of five cairns in a line, some of which are now only a large pile of pebbles, but others having stone burial chambers that can be entered. The site is far more interesting than it looks from the air. Nether Largie north cairn, seen in the foreground, contains a burial chamber which can be entered from the top, and inside is a stone burial cist which has a capstone with cup and ring marks and carvings of axe heads on it.

In addition to the five aligned cairns, there are other cairns close by, as well as cup and ring marked rocks and a stone circle.

Knockfarrel Vitrified Fort, Highland

Fine examples of vitrified stone can be seen all around the plateau on top of Knockfarrel hill which was fortified in the Iron Age. Vitrification is believed to have occurred when the ramparts made of wood and stone were burnt, presumably when the fort was attacked, and Knockfarrel is one of the best places to find vitrified rock, especially along the southern rampart.

Two folktales were told about Knockfarrel, one of them involving fire. Both tales featured the giants who were believed to live on the hill. In the first, the giants were hunting on the Isle of Skye when they saw flames and, fearing for the safety of their families, hastened home just in time to rescue their wives who had been shut in a hut which was then set on fire by their enemies. The other tale is about a stone-throwing competition between a giant and a dwarf. The giant threw a stone carved with an eagle over to Fodderty, whereupon the dwarf picked up the two huge stone gateposts of the fort and hurled them after the eagle stone. The first story was probably told as an explanation for all the vitrified rock that people had found on Knockfarrel. In addition to its archaeological interest, Knockfarrel fort also provides a terrific viewpoint over the surrounding countryside.

*Loanhead of Daviot
Recumbent Stone Circle,
Aberdeenshire*

This recumbent stone circle
is similar to the one at Easter
Aquhorthies (see p. 111) in having
a huge stone lying on its side
between two upright stones.
Although this feature is the most
prominent peculiarity of this site,
other interesting features were
discovered during an excavation
earlier this century.

The circle of eight standing
stones and the recumbent setting,
68 feet (20.5 metres) in diameter,
enclose a ring cairn of small
boulders, and other smaller cairns
had been built around the standing
stones. The site may have been in
use throughout the Bronze Age and
into the early Iron Age, though the
nature of its use may have changed
during this long period. It could
initially have been a ritual site
involving astronomical observations,
as apparently all the recumbent
stone circles were – then it could
later have been a burial site, judging
by the cairns. A complex and
intriguing place, whose secrets are
likely to remain lost forever.

Torhouse Stone Circle, Dumfries and Galloway

Torhouse stone circle in south-west Scotland is many miles from the recumbent stone circles in Aberdeenshire (see, for example, Easter Aquhorthies stone circle, p. 111), yet it is vaguely similar in that three stones are grouped together. However the similarity may be nothing more than coincidence, as the three stones here are not part of the circle's circumference as in Aberdeenshire. At Torhouse, nineteen granite boulders make up an attractive small circle, with the three stones inside and a possible ruined burial cairn close to them. In the seventeenth century the central stones were known as King Galdus's Tomb.

Traprain Law Hillfort, East Lothian

Sitting like a beached whale on the flat countryside, Traprain Law would have been an impregnable fortress throughout the 1,000 years it was occupied. Sadly, the north-east section is now being quarried away: modern man achieves with his powerful machinery what defeated all earlier raiders.

The remains of ramparts are all that can be seen today of the hill's turbulent history, and archaeological excavation has established that the size and outline of the fort were altered several times during its occupation. Various finds have helped to bring the past to light. Pottery cremation urns suggest possible occupation around 1500 BC, while bronze axes, knives, spears and other items probably date to the sixth and seventh centuries BC. A hoard of Roman silverware had been buried in a pit: it comprised pieces of over 100 objects such as plates, bowls and spoons, all cut up ready for melting down.

Traprain Law was the capital of the Votadini tribe during the first few centuries AD, the fortress being abandoned when they left around the middle of the fifth century. According to folklore, Traprain Law was also the capital of King Loth, the hero of Lothian: only 300 yards (300 metres) to the south-west is a standing stone 8 feet (2.5 metres) tall, which was known as the Loth Stone.

White Caterthun and Brown Caterthun Hillforts, Angus

Impressively defended by double stone walls up to 10 feet (3 metres) high, the White Caterthun Iron Age hillfort in Angus is visually more dramatic than its neighbour, the Brown Caterthun three-quarters of a mile (1.2 kilometres) away, although the latter has several lines of defences encircling its hilltop site. The White Caterthun has the remains of a rock-cut cistern, which is 10 feet (3 metres) deep, inside it. Among the stone walls to the west there is also a 6-foot (3-metre) boulder with around seventy cupmarks (prehistoric carvings) on it. According to folklore, all the stones for the White Caterthun's defences were brought here in a witch's apron in a single morning.

WALES

Wales is a mountainous country, a fact reflected in the type of prehistoric remains which can be seen today. They are invariably built of stone: even the hillforts usually have stone ramparts rather than the earth banks more usually seen in England. The people of the Iron Age were not afraid to tame even the wildest mountain tops – and the reward is amazing views as well as near-impenetrable fortresses. It might be argued that the latter would be more important to the builders than the former, but judging from the prehistoric art which survives, it is probably safe to say that they were not insensitive to the grandeur and beauty of the natural world. It is difficult to pick out some hillforts as being more impressive than others, but personal choice would favour Dinas Bran and Pen-y-Gaer.

Burial chambers built of large stones are also numerous in Wales, and the settings are again noteworthy. Pentre Ifan has beauty in the delicate balance of the stones, while Carreg Samson has a fine coastal situation. Cairns of smaller stones are also frequently seen in rocky Wales: Arthur's Stone with views out over land and sea is especially noteworthy, but none can beat Gop Cairn for its size (it is comparable to Silbury Hill), and in addition there are coastal views from the top.

Major stone circles and standing stones are surprisingly less numerous in Wales than in England, but perhaps many have been lost: the stones once fallen would be unnoticeable among the rocks naturally littering the landscape. Also, there is little point in photographing from the air a standing stone in a stony setting! But a good guidebook will pinpoint those worth searching for.

One thing that Wales is rich in is atmosphere. It is impossible to choose between the sites which are illustrated in this book, since the atmosphere at any site will vary according to the weather, in addition to other more subtle influences, but for us a special place is Din Lligwy settlement on the island of Anglesey. In a small grassy clearing surrounded by trees are the remains of nine stone huts, and in this place the lives of our unknown ancestors were played out. Their existence must have left some indefinable influence on this small patch of ground, in addition to the purely physical remains of their homes.

Dinas Bran Hillfort, Denbighshire

Moel ty Uchaf Stone Circle

Arthur's Stone/Maen Ceti Burial Chamber, Swansea

Sited up on the moors of the Gower Peninsula, with distant sea views, Arthur's Stone at the right of the photograph is the possible remains of a Neolithic burial chamber, though it doesn't fit any of the known categories established by archaeologists. The capstone, now broken, would have weighed 30–5 tons. Not far away, and visible in the photograph as a large heap of stones, is a Bronze Age burial cairn. Other smaller heaps of stones on the moor may be the remains of early field clearances.

According to folk belief, the 30-ton capstone was a mere pebble in the shoe of the giant King Arthur, which was irritating him as he went to fight the Battle of Camlann. So he removed it and threw it seven miles (11 kilometres) to its present position. It used to be the custom for young girls from Swansea to leave cakes of barley-meal, honey and milk on Arthur's Stone at midnight when there was a full moon. They then crawled round the stone three times on hands and knees, hoping to see their sweethearts. If they appeared, their fidelity was proved, but if not, then the girls knew that the boys did not intend to marry them.

Bryn Celli Ddu Chambered Cairn, Anglesey

Bryn Celli Ddu on the Isle of Anglesey is a Neolithic burial chamber, but it was built on the site of an earlier henge monument (a circular earthwork used for ceremonial purposes in Neolithic times, similar to Avebury and Stonehenge, though not necessarily so elaborate). This is an important archaeological site, but it is unfortunate that it is not located in a more appropriate setting. It looks sadly out of place, as if arbitrarily set down in the middle of twentieth-century farmland.

Nevertheless it is a magical place. The stone burial chamber is still intact under the covering earth mound, and can be entered along a 25-foot (7.5-metre) passage. Inside the chamber is an enigmatic standing stone: they are not usually found inside burial chambers, and its function here is completely unknown. There is also a strange meandering carving on a stone outside the tomb.

Caer Euni, Gwynedd

Only a few miles from the previous
site, Caer Drewyn, is another fine
hillfort, Caer Euni, just over the
border in Gwynedd. As with most
hillforts in Wales, it commands
magnificent views over the
surrounding countryside. Deep
rock-cut ditches provided
protection to the fort's Iron Age
inhabitants, their presence being
suggested by the dark patches
inside the fort which may indicate
the sites of houses or rubbish
pits. An intriguing discovery inside
the outer ditch was evidence of
vitrified rock, which is believed
to occur when a stone and timber
rampart is destroyed by fire. Such
vitrified rock is usually found only
in Scottish forts (see, for example,
Knockfarrel, p. 116), so its presence
here is very unusual, and the
mystery is only likely to be solved
if an archaeological excavation
is undertaken.

Caer Drewyn Hillfort, Denbighshire

Overlooking Corwen and the important Dee valley in south Denbighshire, this hilltop was a natural site for a hillfort, and Caer Drewyn dates from the Iron Age. Traditionally it was said to have been the settlement of Gwyn ap Nudd, King of the Fairies; but Drewyn was also said to be the name of a giant, with the fort being a cattle enclosure used by his wife as the place to milk her cows. Because of the strong local association with the great Welsh hero Owain Glyndwr (Owen Glendower being his anglicized name), who was said to have been born and lived in the Corwen area, Caer Drewyn was naturally linked to his exploits, and was said to be the place where he gathered his army together.

Capel Garmon Neolithic Burial Chamber, Conwy

Capel Garmon Neolithic burial chamber was sited in a spot with fine view across the mountains of Snowdonia, sadly not visible in the photograph. The stone burial chamber is now open to view, but would originally have had a covering of earth or stones on top of the large roofing slabs, one of which (14 feet/4.3 metres long) survives.

The entrance into the tomb was from the side, and what looks like an entrance at the eastern end is in fact a false entrance, similar to that at Belas Knap (see p. 23). Ceremonies may have been held in the forecourt in front of this false entrance (top of photograph). The entrance into the western end was made in the last century when the tomb was used as a stable.

Carreg Samson/Long House Burial Chamber, Pembrokeshire

Known as Carreg Samson or Long House, this Neolithic burial chamber on the Pembrokeshire coast was used earlier this century as a sheep-shelter, the farmer having blocked up the holes between the seven upright stones. The large capstone is supported on only three of the uprights. It is assumed that originally the whole structure would have been covered with earth, but there is no surviving evidence that it ever was.

Craig Rhiwarth Hillfort,
Powys

This forbidding rocky mountainside
looks the most unlikely place to set
up home, but it must have had
some attraction to the people who
lived in the Berwyn Mountains of
north Powys in the Iron Age, since
the remains of a hillfort have been
found here. Called Craig Rhiwarth,
the steepness of the site meant that
only the north needed defending,
and the defences took the form of a
stone wall, the course of which can
still be traced. The outlines of many
round huts are also still visible, and
they appear to have been
reconstructed, suggesting that the
fort was occupied for a long time.
Rectangular enclosures in the same
area are likely to be the remains of
late medieval sheepfolds. Today the
mountain overhangs the village of
Llangynog, and the valleys are the
only comfortably habitable parts of
the Berwyns. In the Iron Age, either
the weather was better or the
people were a lot hardier than
they are today.

Dinas Bran Hillfort, Denbighshire

Castell Dinas Bran dominates the Vale of Llangollen in south Denbighshire – and what an incredible location this is for a castle! The ruins that can be seen today are of the thirteenth-century castle, but this was built inside an Iron Age hillfort. The name Dinas Bran is intriguing: *dinas* is the Welsh word for city, and Bran was a legendary hero whose buried head King Arthur unwisely exhumed: so long as it remained buried, this island was protected against invasion. Another connection with Arthurian legend is the belief that Dinas Bran is the place where the Holy Grail is hidden. Fairies were said to live on the hill, and a golden harp to be hidden there, which can only be found by a boy whose white dog has a silver eye.

Din Lligwy Settlement, Anglesey

Hidden away on the Isle of Anglesey are the remains of a settlement dating from the early years of the first millennium AD. It is known as Din Lligwy, and the round and rectangular stone buildings were used for different purposes: dwellings, barns, workshops, animal pens. Hearths for iron-working have been found, with heaps of slag; and domestic items such as pottery and glass. This may have been a self-contained country estate, possibly built by a native chieftain in the Roman period. Today, tucked away inside its wood, it is like a window to the past, isolated from the twentieth-century world.

Dyffryn Ardudwy Chambered Cairn, Gwynedd

The sea can be glimpsed on the horizon in this photograph: Dyffryn Ardudwy chambered cairn is only a mile inland from the west coast of Wales. Unusually, it has two separate burial chambers (one under the tree), both on a bed of white boulders, though originally they would have been totally covered by a cairn of boulders. The monument dates from the Neolithic period, and pottery fragments, traces of cremation burials and two stone pendants have been found there.

Foel Trigarn Hillfort, Pembrokeshire

Foel Trigarn means 'Hill of the Three Cairns', aptly named because this hillfort is dominated by three Bronze Age burial cairns up to 10 feet (3 metres) tall. These predate the building of the hillfort, which was occupied over a long period starting in the first millennium BC, and this suggests that the Iron Age people who lived in the fort either respected the cairns as the holy places of their ancestors, or perhaps were more practical and used them as lookout posts. Whatever the reason, they did not dismantle them. Foel Trigarn is made up of three separate defended enclosures, and is perched on top of the eastern summit of the Preseli Hills, a magnificent location high above the surrounding countryside, though it wouldn't be a very good place to choose as a home today. Probably we are less hardy than our Iron Age ancestors, or possibly the weather was somewhat better in those days! But there is no doubt that the fort was occupied, and for a long time. Well over 200 hut sites were discovered during excavations, and all kinds of domestic items were found, including pottery and stone vessels, spindle whorls, jet rings and glass beads.

Gop Cairn, Flintshire

Both date and purpose of the huge Gop Cairn are unknown, though it is certainly the second-largest artificial mound in Britain, beaten only by Silbury Hill in Wiltshire. Standing now around 46 feet (14 metres) high, it may once have been even taller: a dip in the top shows where excavations and stone-robbing have occurred. No trace of human burial has been found in the cairn, only a few animal bones, but it is clearly artificial, and the remains of a wall around the base have been noted. Perhaps the cairn was used for some other purpose than burial. Very close, on the slope below, are caves in the limestone outcrop, only discovered and excavated just over 100 years ago. Traces of occupation from before the end of the last ice age were found, and also the remains of people buried in the Neolithic period. Perhaps the cairn, rather than being Bronze Age as generally assumed, dates from further back in time, and was part of a Neolithic ritual landscape. Much more recently, its size has caused it to be popularly seen as the burial place of some famous person, and it has thus been named as the grave of Boudicca/Boadicea, Queen of the Iceni in the first century AD. It is also said that in 1938 a local man saw ghostly Roman soldiers here one night, and a Roman general on a white horse on Gop Cairn itself.

Moel Arthur Hillfort, Denbighshire

Moel Arthur is a compact Iron Age hillfort, one of several on the hilltops along the Clwydian range, overlooking the Vale of Clwyd (see Pen-y-Cloddiau, p. 149). Although it bears the name 'Arthur's Hill', we know of no surviving folklore that links the place to King Arthur. What folklore does tell us is that treasure was believed to be hidden in a chest inside the fort, the place lit by a supernatural light. But if anyone saw the chest and tried to grab its handle, they would be blown away by a rush of wind. Like Gop Cairn, this is said to be the burial place of Queen Boudicca.

Moel ty Uchaf Stone Circle, Denbighshire
From its position on the slopes of the Berwyn Mountains in south Denbighshire, Moel ty Uchaf stone circle is well sited, overlooking the valleys of the Dee and Alwen rivers. Dated to the Bronze Age, this circle is not like 'normal' stone circles: it is smaller, and a stone found at the centre is thought to have been part of a burial cist (coffin). This could have been covered by an earth mound, with the stone circle acting as a kerb.

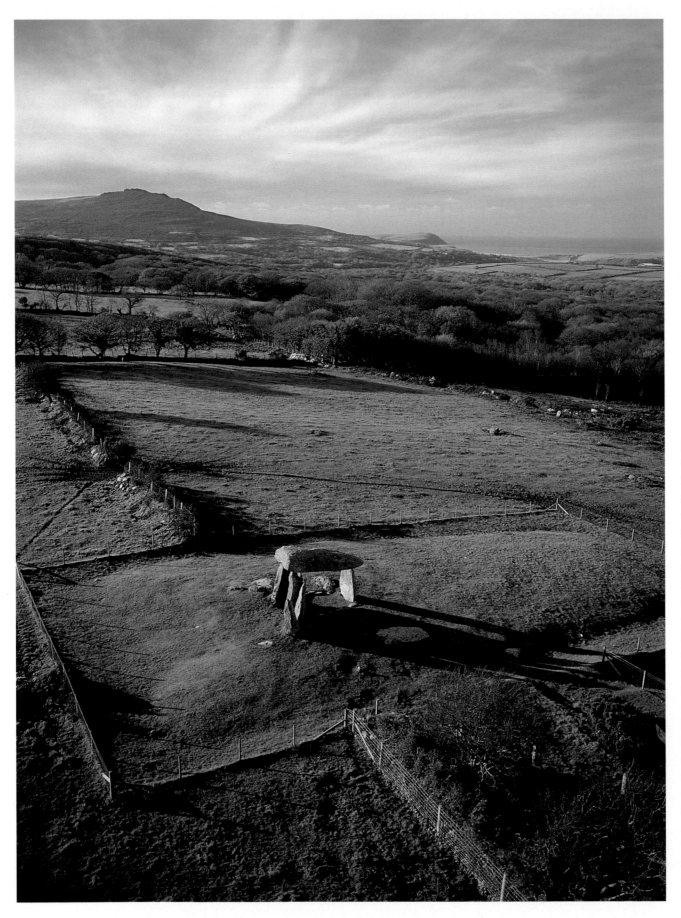

Pentre Ifan Burial Chamber, Pembrokeshire

The mound of earth which once covered Pentre Ifan burial chamber was 130 feet (40 metres) long. In the low winter light, in which the photograph was taken, the mound shows up around the central feature, the stone chamber. This would probably have been hidden, when the Neolithic tomb was in use, but now it is exposed we can see it to be an elegant structure with the 16.5 feet (5 metres) capstone balanced on three of the four uprights. Although the site has been excavated twice, and much learned about the construction of the tomb, very little was found there in the way of artefacts: only a few pieces of pottery and flint, including an arrowhead. In more recent times, Pentre Ifan was said to be a fairy haunt, and they were described as resembling 'little children in clothes like soldiers' clothes and with red caps'.

Pen-y-Cloddiau Hillfort, Denbighshire

Pen-y-Cloddiau is another of the impressive Iron Age hillforts crowning the hilltops along the Clwydian Hills, and is visible from Moel Arthur (see p. 142). The views all around, but especially across the Vale of Clwyd, are spectacular. The outer ramparts are most impressive on the north-east face, as seen here. This fort is more accessible than most others in this area, and the Offa's Dyke long-distance footpath runs through it.

Pen-y-Gaer Hillfort, Conwy

There are so many magnificently sited hillforts in Britain that it is difficult to choose the 'best', but Pen-y-Gaer in its outstanding setting in North Wales must surely be one of the contenders. In clear weather the views are breathtaking – and the Iron Age hillfort is quite interesting too. Stone and earth ramparts encircle the hilltop, and other visible features include circular hut platforms (wooden huts would have been built on these rock bases). Particularly interesting is the *chevaux de frise* near to the entrance. This is an area of closely spaced stones (sometimes sticks were used) placed into the ground and intended to trip up attacking horse or foot soldiers. Despite its commanding position, Pen-y-Gaer is not difficult to reach on foot, once you have found the way in after negotiating a maze of narrow lanes.

Tinkinswood Chambered Barrow, Vale of Glamorgan

The most noticeable feature of Tinkinswood chambered barrow is the huge capstone. Weighing around 40 tons, it is believed to be the largest in Britain. It covered the burial chamber, in which were found the bones of at least fifty people buried here in Neolithic times. Flints and pottery fragments were also found, and bones of sheep, pigs and oxen which may have been the remains of funeral feasts. The funerary rituals may have taken place in the forecourt at the entrance to the tomb. The grassy area around and behind the stones of the burial chamber is also part of the barrow. A depression and piled-up stones mark the site of a pit whose purpose is not known. It has been suggested that it was a place where corpses were left exposed until the flesh had either rotted away or been eaten by birds and animals, after which the bones would be gathered up and interred in the tomb. Knowing this, bad dreams might attend anyone sleeping overnight at the tomb! It was said that anyone sleeping there on the evenings before May Day, St John's Day or Midwinter Day (all significant days in earlier centuries, and maybe also in prehistoric times) would either die, go mad or become a poet!

Tre'r Ceiri Hillfort

Often shrouded in low cloud, which makes it all the more mysterious, the Iron Age hillfort known as Tre'r Ceiri (Town of the Giants) is an impressive place, with the added bonus of spectacular views out over the sea and across the Llyn Peninsula. The remains are equally spectacular: the rampart wall is still 10 feet (3 metres) high, and the remains of more than 150 stone huts still survive, with their walls over 3 feet (1 metre) in height. The wall and huts can be clearly seen in the photograph.

The usage of the hilltop in prehistoric times covers a long period. On the highest point is a Bronze Age burial cairn; this was followed by the fortification of the hilltop in the Iron Age; and there is evidence that the fort was reused by the Romans. Nowadays a site like this would be the last place we would think of living in, so the need for protection against enemies must have been strong in the Iron Age, and in addition the weather may have been better too!

BIBLIOGRAPHY

Ashmore, P. J., *Prehistoric and Bronze Age Scotland* (B. T. Batsford/Historic Scotland, 1996).

Bewley, Robert, *Prehistoric Settlements* (B. T. Batsford/English Heritage, 1994).

Bord, Janet and Colin, *Dictionary of Earth Mysteries* (Thorsons, 1996).

Burl, Aubrey, *The Stonehenge People* (J. M. Dent, 1987).

Burl, Aubrey, *A Guide to the Stone Circles of Britain, Ireland and Brittany* (Yale University Press, 1995).

Castleden, Rodney, *The Stonehenge People* (Routledge, 1987).

Castleden, Rodney, *The Making of Stonehenge* (Routledge, 1993).

Chippindale, Christopher, *Stonehenge Complete* (Thames & Hudson, revised edition 1994).

Cunliffe, Barry, *Wessex to AD 1000* (Longman Group UK, 1993).

Cunliffe, Barry, *Iron Age Britain* (B. T. Batsford/English Heritage, 1995).

Dames, Michael, *The Silbury Treasure* (Thames & Hudson, 1976).

Dames, Michael, *The Avebury Cycle* (Thames & Hudson, 1977).

Dyer, James, *The Penguin Guide to Prehistoric England and Wales* (Penguin Books, 1981).

Dyer, James, *Ancient Britain* (B. T. Batsford, 1990).

Hayes, Andrew, *Archaeology of the British Isles* (B. T. Batsford, 1993).

Hutton, Ronald, *The Pagan Religions of the Ancient British Isles* (Blackwell, 1991).

Malone, Caroline, *Avebury* (B. T. Batsford/English Heritage, 1989).

North, John, *Stonehenge: Neolithic Man and the Cosmos* (HarperCollins, 1996).

Parker Pearson, Michael, *Bronze Age Britain* (B. T. Batsford/English Heritage, 1993).

Richards, Julian, *Stonehenge* (B. T. Batsford/English Heritage, 1991).

Ritchie, Graham and Anna, *Scotland: Archaeology and Early History* (Thames and Hudson, 1981).

Sharples, Niall M., *Maiden Castle* (B. T. Batsford/English Heritage, 1991).

Wainwright, Geoffrey, *The Henge Monuments: Ceremony and Society in Prehistoric Britain* (Thames and Hudson, 1990).

Woodward, Ann, *Shrines and Sacrifice* (B. T. Batsford/English Heritage, 1992).

INDEX

Page numbers in *italics* indicate photographs

First published in the United States of America by
Trafalgar Square Publishing, North Pomfret, Vermont 05053

Printed and bound in Italy

Text copyright © Janet and Colin Bord, 1997
The moral right of Janet and Colin Bord to be identified as the authors of this work
has been asserted in accordance with the Copyright, Designs and Patents Act of 1988
Photographs copyright © Jason Hawkes, 1997
Design and layout copyright © Weidenfeld & Nicolson, 1997

ISBN 1–57076–102–7
Library of Congress Catalog Number: 97–60926

Designed by: The Design Revolution
Map by: Digital Wisdom
Set in: Garamond